"*I firmly believe, from what I have seen,
that this is the chosen spot of all this earth
as far as nature is concerned.*"

– Luther Burbank (1849-1926)
American Horticulturalist
Sonoma County Resident

Dedicated to the Janover's who have made my presence in Sonoma County possible, especially to grandpa Janover's memory in having the foresight to acquire that land between Hulbert Creek and Lover's Lane in 1941 and to his son Lee Jr. for fortifying "The Cabin" over the years, which is where much of this work originated.

First Edition Printed Spring 1999

ISBN #1-890443-24-7

Library of Congress Catalog Card Number 98-96743

Project Conceived, Designed, Researched, Photographed and Edited by Robert Janover / True Images Photography

Proudly produced and printed in the United States of America.

Published by :
Robert Janover
True Images Photography

555 Fifth St Suite 101   P. O. Box 1928
Santa Rosa CA 95401   Guernewood Park CA 95446
(707) 566-0984   (707) 869-3822

www.robertjanover.com
E-mail:janover@sonic.net

Table of Contents

Beauty Everywhere;

North

West

Central

East

South

4

"... The sea, once it casts its spell,
holds one in its net of wonder forever."

– Jacques - Yves Cousteau (1910 - 1997)
(French Marine Explorer)

Duncan's Landing

The Dramatic Coast

Our dramatic coastline beckons and humbles, astonishes and infatuates one with a sense of wonder. Alternating between accessible long sandy beaches with sheer jagged bluffs created by millions of years of the dancing wind and water upon the edge of this continent, the scenes are dazzling. This isn't "Baywatch" beach country, but perhaps one of the most beautiful sections of accessible coastline in California, possibly even the world. The rich waters are cold and deep as the continental shelf drops off rapidly here to become the ocean floor.

Wide-ranging personalities, both natural and man-made, are to be discovered around each curve of State Highway 1 along the seventy-six mile coastline. Numerous road-side beaches, hiking trails, bird and wildlife sanctuarys, picturesque coastal towns and villages with some oddly-funky to ultra modern homes are perched upon these pacific coast cliffs.

Stretching from the southern boarder with Marin County near Bodega Bay and meandering through the hillside town of Jenner, where the Russian River greets the ocean, all the way north to the Sea Ranch community at the border with Mendocino County, the drive is spectacular. Access to the harbor seals year-round home at Goat Rock State Beach, abalone diving, surf-boarding, charter cruises, several golf courses, tide-pooling, horseback-riding and the thrill of the seasonal whale migration all enrich the coastal experience. Kruse Rhododendron Preserve, Salt Point State Park, Stillwater Cove Regional Park, the awe-inspiring Buddhist temple high in the hills of western Sonoma County, and the Indian community at Plantation, are some of the rare and unique characteristics of this special area. To see it from the air magnifies the enjoyment of this Pacific coastline.

Aerial North of Salmon Creek

Coastline North of Wrights Beach

North Coast at Sea Ranch

Goat Rock at Jenner

Harbor Seals, Seagulls, Mussels, Barnacles, and Starfish (Sea Stars)

"I have a strange longing for the great simple
primeval things, such as the sea, to me no less of a
mother than the earth."

– Oscar Wilde (1854-1900)
Irish Writer

The Restored Russian Outpost of Fort Ross

Goat Rock at Twilight

"The clearest way into the universe
is through a forest wilderness."
– John Muir (1838-1914)
Scottish Born-American Naturalist

Armstrong Redwoods State Reserve and Surroundings

The Redwoods

"Sequoia sempervirens", The Coast Redwood Trees are the world's tallest living things and are ever-present in western Sonoma County. Today's mighty redwoods are impressive with many standing over 200 feet tall and an occasional old growth survivor rises to over 300 feet and are up to 2,000 years old. As inspiring as today's stands are, they are mere babies compared to the old growth redwoods that the early American settlers of the 1860's witnessed. The flatlands around Guerneville once contained the thickest groves of redwood trees that may have ever existed. So thick and dark were some areas that it is said the local indians shunned them as the dwelling place of evil spirits.

Lumber operations in the region began in 1865. In 1873 the largest known tree in the world measuring 367 feet and 8 inches was felled along the banks of Fife Creek, in what is now Guerneville. Many trees over 350 feet high and up to 14 feet in diameter carpeted the area. Early-day loggers found these trees yielded 180,000 to 200,000 board feet of extremely high quality lumber. This volume and proximity to San Francisco via the newly established train lines ensured the harvesting of the local redwoods. The city of San Francisco was built with Sonoma County redwoods, not once, but also a second time after the 1906 earthquake and fires leveled the growing city-by-the-bay.

In 1916 residents voted to preserve sections of the redwoods as parks. Armstrong Redwoods State Reserve and the Austin Creek State Recreation Aréa are excellent examples of the success of the early environmental movement and the emerging knowledge for the need to slow the cutting of these wondrous trees. Today, an astute and intense environmentalism exists in many souls of western Sonoma County and every attempt to cut even a single redwood is aggressively met with opposition from those who wear their "tree-hugger" label loudly and proudly.

Redwoods Found Around Guerneville

Sunrise at Rio Nido

"It is a remarkably pleasant occupation to lie on one's back in a forest and look upwards! It seems that you are looking into a bottomless sea that is stretching out far and wide below you.

Guerneville, including a very rare albino redwood tree with striped variegated leaves (detail) in Guernewood Park.

"Invest in the millennium. Plant Sequoias."

– Wendell Berry (b.1934)
Kentucky Farmer and Writer

Sunrise in Armstrong Woods

Clouds over Redwood Lined Hills of Forestville

"Every moment Nature starts on the longest journey,
and every moment she reaches her goal."

– Johann Wolfgang von Goethe (1749-1832)
German Poet

The Russian River

Shabaikai, "Big Snake" as named by the Native Indians. Slavianka, "Little Beauty" as the Russians called it. El Rio de San Ignacio, "The River of St. Ignatius" as referred to by Captain Luis Arguello when he discovered its upper reaches in the area north of Cloverdale in 1821. American settlers recognized the influence of the Russians who had established a fur-trading colony at Fort Ross on the coast north of Jenner from 1812 through 1841 and thus its name today.

Beautiful and moody, glistening and sullen, the Russian River could possible be one of the hottest and more complex political and environmental issues to face a waterway that just wants to quietly meander its way to the ocean. A summertime playground for hundreds of thousands of people and a national winter-time headline grabber with news stories about her periodic tantrums. Floods and reeking havoc on the lives of residents along her banks, creeks and tributaries which feed into the river has been known to occur (the publisher writes somewhat sarcastically having dealt with this personally, multiple times) over the last century. The winters water flow can be 200 times greater than that of the summer volume, though it is gorgeous emerald green in Spring, Summer and Fall with a number of temporary dams in place during the Summer months for recreation and water control. The river is also a drinking water source for 500,000 people in Sonoma and Marin Counties as well as a major source of water for the vast agricultural industry of the region.

Sea otter, and a number of fish species, several of which are now endangered make their home in the river. Steelhead, the coho salmon, bass and trout were all once in abundance, but currently their numbers and size have been greatly diminished. A water shed committee and organizations such as The Friends of the River and others have been organized to address issues and the health of the river. Once taken for granted as a summertime haven, many complex issues now divide a wide range of people, though most realize long-term measures must be taken to ensure that the Russian River is used wisely now and for future generations.

25

Reflection on the Estuary at Jenner

Clouds at Sunset and Reflection at Duncans Mills

Morning Light at Guernewood Park

"What we call the beginning is often the end
And to make an end is to make a beginning.
The end is where we start from."

— T. S. Eliot (1888-1965)
British Born-American Poet

The River Winding Through Alexander V

"Teach your children what we have taught our children – that the earth is our mother.
Whatever befalls the earth befalls the sons and daughters of the earth."
– Chief Seattle (1788-1866)
Squamish Indian Leader

The Russian River
at Wohler Bridge

Sunset From Jenner

"*Good wine is a good familiar creature if it be well used.*"
– Shakespeare (1564-1616)
English Playwright and Poet

Merlot Grapes in Sonoma County

The Wine Country

The Sonoma Wine Country has gain
international recognition and accla
for producing prestigious award w
ning wines over the last several decad
Grapes have become the leading agric
tural crop by producing almost 60%
the total annual harvest in Sono
County. Marketing and promotion of t
county as a major wine producing regi
has been greatly influenced by orga
zations such as the Sonoma Coun
Wineries Association and the establis
ment of the California Welcome Cen
in Rohnert Park. Since 1993 this facil
has offered visitors and residents ali
the opportunity to learn about the loc
wine history and experience the ent
winemaking process through tastin
workshops, classes on food and wi
pairing and informational programs.

Eleven wine appellations exist, produ
ing up to about 190,000 tons of grape
year. 1997's crop was valued at nea
300 million dollars. The Chardonn
grape produces almost two times t
yield as the Cabernet Sauvignon grap
followed closely by Merlot, Pinot N
and Zinfandel as the other prima
grapes harvested here. A host of oth
grapes are grown and many differe
blendings occur to create some intere
ing, complex, unique and superb win
Approximately 145 different winer
are in operation during any given ye
each with its own unique personal
and philosophy regarding winemakin
Many of the wineries offer free tastin
daily, while some request reservatio
for personal tastings and tours. T
meandering country roads lead throu
wonderfully visual landscapes a
architecture that exemplify the Sono
Wine Country setting. Numerous wi
tasting events, sales and promotio
occur throughout the year uniti
wineries, valleys and regions. T
Winter Wonderland event, select bar
tastings, round-robin tastings, t
Harvest Auction, and the Harvest F
celebration in October which showcas
the years local award winning wines a
some of the popular events.

Mustard Wildflowers in a Healdsburg Vineyard

"Who will reap what I have sown in this almighty sweet land?"
                                        – Jack London

Aerial of Vineyards and Pond on Sonoma Mountain

Aerial of Vineyard Rows in Kenwood

Aerial of Vineyards in Alexander Valley

Late Spring Storm Clouds Over Western Santa Rosa

"Earth is here so kind, that just tickle her with a hoe
and she laughs with a harvest."

– Douglas Jerrold (1803-1857)
English Humorist and Journalist

Zinfandel Grapes in the Hills of the Russian River Valley

Zinfandel Grapes Ready for Harvest

Russian River Valley

Carneros Region

The Color of the Seasons

Alexander Valley

Sonoma Carneros

Dry Creek Valley

The Fall Colors in Forestville

Appellations of Sonoma County

Alexander Valley

Carneros Region

Chalk Hill

Dry Creek Valley

Green Valley

Knights Valley

Northern Sonoma

Russian River Valley

Sonoma Coast

Sonoma Mountain

Sonoma Valley

Mt. Saint Helena

Geyser Peak

Merced Hills, West of Cotati

"Over all the mountain tops is peace"
Johann Wolfgang von Goethe (1749-1832)
German Poet

Aerial view of the Mayacamas Mountains.
Sugarloaf Ridge at Kenwood (left)
Austin Creek St. Recreation Area (right)

Sonoma County

"I liked those hills up there.
They were beautiful, as you see,
and I wanted beauty."
- Jack London

Bennett Peak at Annadel State Park

The Petaluma Hills

Sonoma Mountain from Glen Ellen
and from Sonoma (right)

Sonoma County

Jack London State Historic Park

Highway 1, North Coast

"My road calls me, lures me
West, East, South and North.
Most roads lead men homewards,
my road leads me forth."

-John Mansfield (1878-1967)

Grove Street, Cotati

Armstrong Woods Road

Dirt Road in a Kenwood Vineyard

Sweetwater Springs Road

Backroads

Sonoma Mt. Road in Spring

Tin Barn Road

West Dry Creek Road

Coleman Valley Road

Sonoma Mt. Road in Fall

"Two roads diverged in a wood,
and I took the one less traveled by,
and that has made all the difference."
-Robert Frost (1874-1963)
American Poet

Wohler Bridge

Balshaw Foot Bridge, Petaluma

Monte Rio Bridge

Hacienda Bridge

Kidd Creek Bridge

Sonoma County

Sonoma Stone Bridge, Julliard Park

Guerneville Bridge

Glen Ellen Bridge

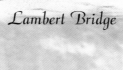

Lambert Bridge

Walking Bridge, Cazadero

Healdsburg Railroad Bridge

A Taste of

Melt-in-your mouth raspberries. Lean and tender fresh meats. Hand-crafted farmstead cheeses. Full-bodied red wines and fresh and fruity whites. These delectable farm products make Sonoma County a culinary mecca—the breadbasket for Bay Area specialty buyers and a destination for those craving hand-crafted food products along with world class wines.

Set in California's Coast Range, a variety of growing conditions offer farmers a palette of varying soils, rainfall, sun and elevation. Small, independent farmers can experiment with techniques to produce quality local products. Family businesses nurture their products with pride and care.

Sonoma County's #1 industry is agriculture, with a measured value of over $2 billion dollars in 1997. Its vineyards have long held claim to a premier spot in California's Wine Country. Other famous products include foie gras, duck, lamb, mushrooms, farm-crafted goat and sheep cheeses, premium vegetables shipped world-wide, sea urchins, Preston Point oysters and a world-class virgin olive oil. Micro-brews, jams, juices, salsas and specialty vegetables share the culinary spotlight.

Many products bear a Sonoma Grown™ and Sonoma Made™ insignia, telling consumers exactly where products orginiate. Select Sonoma County, a non-profit marketing organization founded in 1988, mounts coordinated marketing efforts in local and Bay Area grocery stores.

Sometimes known as the land of "Foodandwine," tasting experiences are at every turn in this region of rolling hill-and-valley topography. Small farms dot the landscape. Look for Sonoma County Farm Trails signs, marking those open to the public. Look for displays of local products at farm stands and retail grocery or speciality stores. And don't miss special events hosted by restaurants and wineries featuring vintners and seasonal foodstuffs.

A Santa Rosa Saloon, 1880
Courtesy, Sonoma County Library

1995 Beerfest

Sonoma County

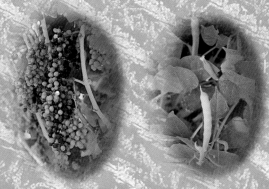

The following pages contain images that are some of my personal favorites and have generated a good deal of interest over the years from the various publications in which they have appeared. Six of the scenes are featured in Sonoma County, the Collection, a group of 18 post cards bound together in a post card book self-published (somehow) during the floods of 1995. Each copy of the 5,000 books is signed and hand-numbered. Various local retailers still carry the book and the individual cards.

Brief descriptions about the photographs origins are included on the following pages, accompanied by some of my own creative writings that were created years ago, mostly, as "stream of consciousness" prose that would come to me very easily and lyrically flowing. With no intention to sit down and write something, it was more like the words were just there and needed to pop out and upon review they seemed to have a real significance to me on several levels. The times the words would appear was rather poignant for I had never studied writings or the written word, wasn't a particularly good student or very prolific at much of anything. The lyricalness of many of the works was intriguing as I had always loved music and it was something that I was becoming more drawn to in those teenage years when we begin to just start to begin to get a vague understanding of who we might be. As that young person starting to wonder about the bigger picture of life and life's challenges, the words that I was writing seemed to be a creative release that was new and fresh and starting to really question the "why's" in my life and they seemed to be musical or visual in nature, at least as I perceived. Sometimes I understood their meanings, other times I was clueless, they were just interesting unstructured ramblings on paper. I began to try to study the structure in writing though, as usual, trying to learn something instead of just doing it proved useless. It was much more interesting to get into that place or mode or mood or whatever space it is that allows the natural creative energy to flow.

The same philosophy seemed to be developing with the growing interest in photography. I was reading about the basic foundations of the photographic process and quickly caught on to the relationship of shutter speed and aperture, especially how a shutter speed could change the look of a scene regarding motion. As I picked up my first roll of slide film (by accident) in 1983 and experienced the actual drama that I believed I was seeing when shooting but not being represented by the color prints I was getting, I made a great step forward in learning and understanding the color photographic process. There was a distinct time in 1984 just after the death of Ansel Adams when my photographic work greatly increased in quality and intensity. I was becoming focused (yes, pun) and quite critical for the first time in my life about something that seemed to matter. By 1986 the passion had kicked in and I got the wild-hair idea to venture out into the world of self-employment as a photographer as a fairly young person. The experience was humbling, devastating, and intensely gratifying. For as involved as things were while "growing up", this finally felt like living and feeling positive and in control of the things happening on a daily basis. This period also overlapped with the writings that were still flowing and I began experimenting with combining the two mediums. 1986 also marked the beginning of a ten year phase in which one relative passed away each year. Within a year from the jump to freelancing I was periodically travelling the country photographing for a post card company, had contracted with Landmark Calendars for the "Moment's" calendar project which combined those creative writings with some of the artsy nature shots I was capturing. Also, a Windham Hill album cover deal was landed, featuring an abstract experimental image created by exposing the film while rewinding the film through the camera, yet another creative idea that had just come to me in the natural creative learning process. I ended up producing six calendars with Landmark through 1993, each having prose accompanied to the photographs but it had become more about trying to write to the visuals for a commercial project someone else had the final say-so about, instead of just letting everything flow together naturally. Over the years I have published several projects combining the words and visuals, including the captioning on the post card and notecard series and had even produced a video of still photos converted to video and scored with some original music co-created with the gifted musician, Chip "Rabbittraxx" Adams, that included the writings and a voice-over. Though "Inspirations' Pulse" never really went anywhere, it was the building block that established a desire to create some complex projects and the challenges in seeing things through. Writing became less of a natural and instinctive process as the photography became more and more intense and involved which deepened the passion for capturing an ultimate scene. So... years later and I'm doing what still feels natural though still having periodic bouts of the starving artist syndrome.

My youthful wonderings have turned to wandering and watching. To date, brief photo trips to 38 states and Canada have been achieved, though it's Sonoma County I continue to come home to and the images in this "Gallery" section are part of the reason why. The creative writings are generally excerpts from longer lyrical pieces.

RCJ

The gallery section is dedicated to the memories of the five acquaintances that passed away during the production of this book, including Colonel Pete who passed at the very end of this production and who had come into the Janovers lives just as my photography was beginning. "Be sure to give ann that hug, pete."

The Gallery

"Art never expresses anything but its self."
– Oscar Wilde (1854-1900)

"Living is my job and my art."
– Michel de Montaigne (1533-1592)

*"My eyes were finally opened and I understood
nature: I learned at the same time to love it."*
– Monet (1840-1926)

The impressionistic quality to this photo was created by the use of Agfachrome® 200 film push processed to ASA 800 to accentuate the grain. Additionally, a small amount of hair spray was applied to a filter to add a softening effect. The last bit of technique was pretty low-tech...this was photographed through my vehicles raindrop dotted window which adds some subtle and select diffusion. This barn is located along River Road and has become a classic for artists renditions. A Minolta x-700 camera with a 50mm lens was used.

Before the vines, we view
the beauty youth can be
in a winter scene.
Before the vines,
we view
the host...rediscovery,
like babies of today,
we are but
vines awaiting fruit
RCJ

A rather routine looking sunset started becoming more and more golden in color as the earth rolled away from the sun and the atmospheric haze created the partially disappearing sun. A shutter speed of $1/2$ of a second captured just enough motion to give this photo an intriguing painterly feel. No filters or color enhancements were used. Shot with a Mamiya 645 1000s with a 210mm lens on Fujichrome® 50 film.

Life,
It moves in rhythm
The wave,
It is a friend
And the silence can be moving
Waving to a friend.

RCJ

After a less than interesting class at the Junior College, walking back to my vehicle I noticed the beginning of some color in the puff clouds overhead. Walking under these impressive oaks quite often, I had always seen the potential for some great shots with the right lighting. A quick dash to the truck and back left only about 30 seconds to shoot off a quick roll of Fujichrome® 50 of this rapidly changing scene before all the color was gone from the sky. It was at this point I decided I wasn't able to learn as much in the classroom as I could in spending more time learning outside in the "real world" classroom, proving once again to myself that self-education was the only true learning I seemed capable of. Photographed with a Mamiya 645 1000s and 45mm lens (from a very awkward position!).

To color in the skies
with an open mind's eye
is to see all that you can
and enjoy what you like.

RCJ

I've had about ten people claim to be the little fisher person in this shot. Truth is, I didn't even notice the person until getting the films back and evaluating them. A quarter mile from the cabin, I pass this scene daily and it changes in appearance every morning. This photo was taken when I had a regular 9-5pm "real job" and was rushing to work when I noticed the sun popping through the fog with some great colors. Back home to get the equipment and back to the scene within a couple of minutes, the sun was still flickering in and out of the fog. Within about three minutes the fog had overtaken the sun and the scene was left in cold monochromatic gray hews. The figure in this scene just capped the serene and contemplative feeling and gave scale and size to the setting. A Mamiya 6 x 9 cm camera was used with a 100mm lens, shot on Fujichrome® 50 film.

The sight of silence
understands this moment's meaning
and asks me to stay
awhile.

RCJ

This image is an example of a technique I've used periodically since about 1990/91. Understanding the traditional darkroom techniques of burning and dodging, I began experimenting with that technique to achieve a similar effect on the actual original image in-camera, on the transparency film rather than after-the-fact in the darkroom while printing on paper. Experienced at the math needed to figure out exposures lead me to explore ways to balance scenes like this one where an extreme range of exposure values are contained within a single scene but films limited latitude to capture that range of lightness and darkness with a traditional exposure would always result in either overexposed or underexposed areas. True to my sometimes abstract ways, I started taking photographs holding my fingers over portions of the lens in an attempt to balance the exposure needed in one place with that of another. These exposures were generally between $^1/_2$ a second and 15 seconds and because the mirror in the camera locks-up during the exposure, the scene would be concealed in the viewfinder, so allot of guesswork and estimating was involved. Needless to say, much film was sacrificed, though once results like this image began to be achieved I felt like I had wandered into some interesting area as I had never heard of this being done. Graduated neutral density filters would give a similar effect though with a limited range and only with a straight line gradation. Some of these images require up to a ten stop range from the highlights to the shadow areas (technical stuff, I know, sorry to those who don't understand the terminology...translation = "a pretty cool technique"). Using the hands allows specific areas of the scene to be manipulated though it is very difficult to get accurate results and generally these scenes are changing so rapidly that a limited number of exposures are possible. Nowadays, Abobe Photoshop® and other software programs allow an unlimited array of image manipulation and a number of people think this is a computer generated image because of the extreme drama, but this is actually how the original transparency looks. While I'm far from being a puritan regarding photographic images, I do stand by the philosophy of "don't mess with Mother Nature" when it comes to nature photography verses digital representations of landscapes. There is something very gratifying in the challenge of achieving an ultimate scene on an original transparency rather than adjusting a natural scene pixel-by-pixel digitally. I do understand the modern technology and embrace it at times for design purposes (as shown in portions of this book with some of the applied digital effects), but with nature scenes, its much more personal to achieve the results in-camera. A Mamiya 654 1000s camera and 80mm lens were used with Fujichrome® 50 film. The sky was exposed for about a second and the lower portion remained being exposed for about 12 seconds.

I received a call, a message on life
I hung up knowing more, but not exactly what
I sat beside myself, and hung my thoughts to dry
I wondered what to wonder, all this magic in the sky.

RCJ

A minute-long exposure about an hour after sunset created this surreal scene at Duncans Landing. That is water and mist from the ocean instead of fog as some people have thought. This was a very cold and windy setting and I was trying to shield the camera and tripod with my body and opened coat as much as possible. I didn't hold out much hope that the unmetered exposures would actually come out so I only shot three photos total of this scene. The dazzling result of the one image that did came out re-invigorated my confidence to trust my instincts and to work through the obstacles. Photographed with a (wet) Mamiya 6 x 9 cm camera and 100mm lens using Fujichrome® 50 film.

Those whose thoughts
Walk on the rocks
Will walk with care
To get to there . . .
The place where conscious
Greets her peers.

RCJ

I'm not really sure if this result was from the use of a close-up lens, bellows, a magnifying filter set or a reversing ring, as I was experimenting with a number of close-up techniques early on. The natural textures and colors in nature hold endless photographic opportunities in the potential to evoke any one of numerous responses. The natural sensualness of a rose is further enhanced by exploring the visual abstracts in the details, up-close. Photographed with a Minolta x-700 on Kodachrome® 64 film.

"In a way, nobody sees a flower really, it is so small, we haven't time -
and to see takes time, like to have a friend takes time."
– Georgia O'Keeffe (1887-1986)
American Painter

Petal Peace
up close and personal,
to see
is like to have a friend
up close and personal
with time, with a friend
up close and personal
to see, is a friend
up close, and to understand
its personal
something not to forget
the specialness of, up close
and personal.
Petal Peace... it's a comforting friend,
when you have the time, and the sight to understand.
RCJ

This is another example of the in-camera dodging/burning technique to balance the exposure of the sky and the foreground. Frantically driving back and forth on River Road while this sky was developing, I wasn't finding any accessible subject matter to include in the foreground with these clouds, so I was about to stop and just shoot the colorful details of the clouds themselves, when finally I came across this patch of red vineyards and the silhouetted trees. This was an instant I knew I would have to try to balance the exposure in the camera because the lighting was too extreme for a traditional exposure. Even knowing this and beginning to calculate the exposures while setting up the tripod, the color in the sky was rapidly fading. Three pictures were all I was able to shoot before the clouds were gray and only this one was exposed anywhere near useable, but again, once I saw this result it was sort of chilling at the potential of this technique. A Mamiya 6 x 9 cm camera and a 150mm lens were used with Fujichrome® 50 film. The overall exposure was about ten seconds with the upper portion of the lens covered at about one second for the sky area.

The traveller
in the corridor of the mind
bumps against on old rivet
and out drops
a wonderful thought
RCJ

"I dream'd in a dream I saw a city invincible to
the attacks of the whole rest of the earth.
I dream'd that was the new city of friends."

– Walt Whitman (1819-1892)
American Poet

*Johnson's Beach during the
Russian River Jazz Festival.*

The Communities

Nine cities, numerous small towns, villages and isolated communities give visual charm and diversity to this county. Approximately 450,000 residents are spread out fairly nicely over 1,026,000 acres, though large plots of agricultural land make up much of the county's acreage while other areas are filled with people and buildings, while still other sections are neither fertile nor inhabitable.

Santa Rosa is the county seat and central in location with about 136,000 residents, making it the most populated city. Highway 101 is the lifeline of the county running north and south and intersects with Highway 12 at downtown Santa Rosa. These two roads link virtually all the main communities in the county. The routes between the towns follow many of the original pioneer-day trails the oxen and horse and carriage would traverse. Locomotive tracks were laid during the 1860's and 70's making transportation much more effective then in turn, the introduction of the automobile made civilian travel on the trains almost obsolete by the late 1930's.

The quiet, slow-paced, atmosphere of the smaller towns, counters with the hustle-and-bustle and related sights and sounds of today's larger cities. This unique and diverse visual personality of the county is appreciated and enjoyed by many of the residents and visitors. Convenience and proximity of most town centers is enhanced by the ability to travel for only several minutes in any direction and be "in the country".

New construction is changing the face of the county, much of it by the development of residential lots, adding more people into smaller clusters of land, while numerous commercial building developments are becoming visible in each town along the Highway 101 corridor. Agencies such as the Agricultural and Preservation Open Space District and the Sonoma Land Trust have been created to counter the potential overdevelopment of the county by acquiring local lands to remain as open space, void of building developments ...forever.

Tourism affects most of the communities by the seasonal influx of millions of visitors and many locals find their employment within this industry. Retail, government, manufacturing and health care are the largest of the job providers.

Sonoma County is still an inviting and popular place to live, work and play, though it has become fairly expensive to live here as rental vacancy rates are very low while median house prices are well above the state average. Each community is unique with their own historical significance and modern influences... where well preserved victorian architecture and family farms coexist with the modernization of the twentieth and twenty-first century's developments.

EMPIRE BUILDING

Aerial View of Downtown

Twilight from Fountaingrove

Horse races at the Fairgrounds

Vineyards, Western Santa Rosa

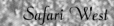

Safari West

Church of One Tree, Built 1875

Fourth and Mendocino, July 4th, 1889
Courtesy, Sonoma County Library

Sonoma Co. Museum, The Original Post Office

Restored Depot, Built 1904

The county seat for Sonoma County, Santa Rosa is 38 square miles containing about 136,000 people in this diverse and thriving economy. Originally established by a Mexican land grant held by Dona Maria Carrillo, the western movement of Missouri farmers and frontiersmen as well as others lead to Santa Rosa's incorporation in 1869. The arrival of the railroad in 1870 would ensure expansive growth for this centrally located city. Today's downtown area, the McDonald Avenue mansions, and historic Railroad Square are all excellent examples that pay homage to the turn-of-the-century era of victorian buildings and a simpler time. The city still contains many relics of yesterday lending an interesting atmosphere to the rural charm and a bigger city sophistication that is somewhat inherited from her big-sister, San Francisco, an hour to the south. A combination of tourism, financial services, manufacturing, electronics, health care and retail sales contribute a large part to the business economy.

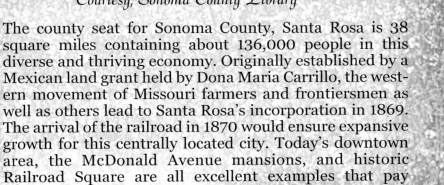

Fountaingrove Round Barn

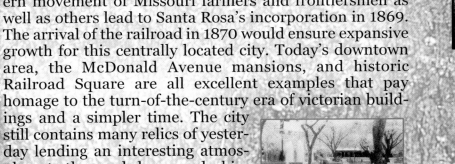

Downtown

Luther Burbank Home and Gardens

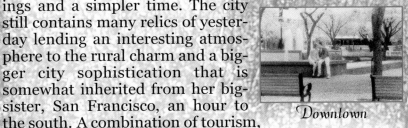

Luther Burbank Center for the Arts

The Gables, Built 1877

Bennett Peak / Annadel St. Park

Hotel La Rose, Railroad Square 75

PETALUMA

Aerial of the River and Eastern Petaluma

Sonoma Mt. Road at Twilight

Barn and Pasture Land

Downtown

McNear Building Detail

Main St. North of Washington, 1906
Courtesy, Sonoma County Library

St. Vincent De Paul's

Library and Museum

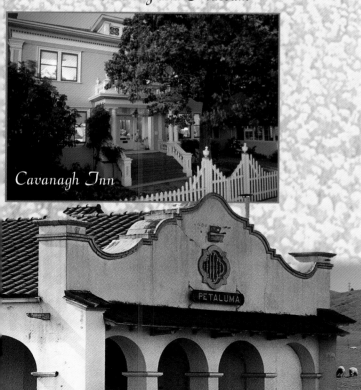

Cavanagh Inn

The Old Adobe, Restored to the 1840's

One of the best preserved American victorian towns, Petaluma today still embraces it's All-American charm with magnificently preserved architecture, acres of open space, rolling hills and active farm lands. Coastal Miwok for "flat back hill", Petaluma was once the site of a large indian village. Incorporated in 1858, the town was one of the few to escape virtually unscathed by the 1906 earthquake which leveled Santa Rosa to the north and San Francisco to the south. Today's city measures 13.3 square miles and has about 50,000 residents. The transformation from being one of California's largest cities in 1860, to becoming the world's egg basket in the early 1900's, to celebrity status  as a feature film and T.V. commercial location starting in the 1970's has not swayed this town from her roots. Parades and celebrations are well organized and very popular with a respect for the past, evident today even as the city continues to develop and expand.

Balshaw Bridge Reflection

Marina

The Old Depot, Built 1914

77

Sonoma

Aerial of Town, Southward View

Bear Flag Revolt Statue

Blue Wing Inn Detail

Downtown Adobes

SEBASTIANI BUILDING.
1933

THEATRE SEBASTIANI THEATRE

Sonoma Valley / Carenos Region

City Hall

Sebastiani Arch

Depot Museum

Swiss Chalet at General Vallejo's Home

Sonoma Plaza, 1872
Courtesy, Sonoma County Library

The Town of Sonoma lies at the base of the Sonoma Valley only 45 minutes north of the Golden Gate Bridge and San Francisco, but worlds away in character. Many layers of history abound in this small town of 8,800-plus residents who play host to over a million visitors a year to the Sonoma Valley. The 8-acre central plaza is the largest of it's kind in California and was the work of General Mariane Guadalupe Vallejo in 1834. 200 trees line the plaza which also contains duck ponds and is bordered with well preserved and restored historical structures *Farmer's Market* including old adobe buildings. Revitalized 19th century hotels and the former Mexican Army Barracks built in 1836 to house General Vallejo's troops are some of the classic structures that hold the memories and echo's of the past. Today's wine industry is very strong here.

Carneros Region

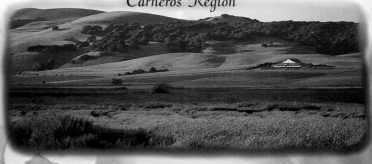

Sonoma Mission, Built 1823

Barrack's Detail

Sears Point Raceway

Buena Vista

Overview from Fitch Mountain

World War Two
Memorial Statue

Museum

West Street, 1872
Courtesy, Sonoma County Library

Villa Chanticleer

Healdsburg Inn on the Plaza

Jordan Vineyard and Winery

Built around a Spanish-styled plaza, the actual Healdsburg city limit is only 3.5 square miles. A rich historical heritage is preserved in the numerous turn-of-the-century victorians and the small-town charm that is still present at the turn-of-the-millennium. Settled in 1852 and incorporated in 1867, this area is the former site of the 48,000 acre Rancho Soyotome land grant that was held by the Yankee sea captain Henry Delano Fitch. Harmon Heald, a native Ohioan founded the area for trading in the 1840's and later the town was named after him. A mediterranean-type climate has helped to yield quality agricultural products since the 1800's. This was once the home of the "Triplets"; prunes, grapes and hops reigned. Today, some 60 wineries are within 15 minutes of the plaza which contains a wide variety of quaint shops, restaurants, antique dealers, and friendly accommodations.

At The Hop Kiln Winery

Ferrari-Carano Winery

Camellia Inn, Built 1869

Madrona Manor, Built 1881

Dry Creek Vineyard

BODEGA BAY

Just north of the coastal border with Marin County lies this picturesque fishing village. Home to about 200 commercial fishing boats, the area was discovered by Lt. Juan Francisco de la Bodega y Cuarda on board the ship Sonora. The rich fishing waters have been an attraction since the days of the Miwok and Pomo Indians. 1962 brought fame to the region with the filming of Alfred Hitchcock's "The Birds". Tourism thrives now with direct beach access, shops, art galleries, inns, boating and recreation.

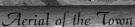

Aerial of the Town

The Potter Schoolhouse, Built 1873
Site of "The Birds" Movie

St. Theresa's Church

WHALE HEAD BONE

The Harbor

Aerial of Bodega Head and Doran Beach

Abrams House Inn, Built 1872

United Church of Cloverdale

Shelford House Inn, Built 1880's

Historical Society Museum

West Street, 1870
Courtesy, Sonoma County Library

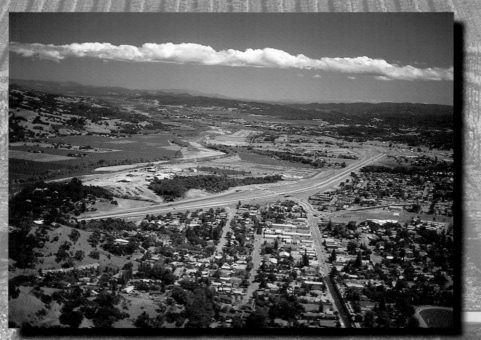

Southeast Aerial View

Downtown Buildings

WELCOME TO

Cloverdale

GATEWAY TO
WARM SPRINGS DAM

6,200 residents enjoy the warmest of micro-climates, here at the top of Alexander Valley. This old stagecoach stop was originally part of the Rancho Rincon de Muscalon grant and was first known as Markle's Place. Once the northernmost citrus growing region in California, the town still celebrates it's Citrus Fair each February. The old-town feel is accentuated with modern influences in a progression from that of a lumber based economy to a tourism related one. Wineries, nearby Lake Sonoma and the Russian River are popular with locals and tourists alike.

Aerial of Lake Sonoma

83

This victorian revival village was the 1880's destination for the North Coast Pacific Railway and today the old train depot is a museum show-casing artifacts from the rail-road's heyday. Founded in 1852 by Alexander and Sam Duncan who ran a sawmill here, the tiny town is now home to unique shops, art gal-leries, a general store and a deli, all set in a classic old-west style along the Russian River.

Northward Aerial View of Duncans Mills

Jenner By The Sea, 1929
Courtesy, Sonoma County Library

A little jewel of a location perched the cliffs where the Russian Riv meets the Pacific Ocean. More th 200 spotted harbor seals make th home here as do an increasing numb of sea otter. Once part of the Mu Rancho, Jenner is named for Char Jenner who arrived around 18 Ever-changing weather cycles c ate ongoing visual treats.

Jenner Inn

North Shore Rail Car

Shops on the North Side of Highway 116

Museum and Stores

Aerial of Jenner, The Russian River and Pacific Ocean at Goat Rock St. Beach

The Parlor at Jenner Inn

Harbor Seals at the Mouth of the River

Aerial of Downtown Forestville

A small community spread out from the Russian River and the redwoods, expanding southward towards Sebastopol. Home of El Molino High School, numerous organic farms producing a wide range of agricultural products and the YA-KA-AMA indian educational center, Forestville was founded by A. J. Forrestville in 1853. This was the terminus of the Petaluma and Santa Rosa Railroad line. Wineries, B & B's and the river gladly play host to visitors.

And Graton

Named for James H. Gray, Graton is revitalizing it's tiny four-corner downtown with modern building fronts, is home to a large wine making facility, a number of restaurants and the National Historical Landmark at the Gravenstein Inn.

Main Street, Graton, 1909
Courtesy, Sonoma County Library

The Farmhouse Inn

Fall Colors

Eastward Aerial View of Graton

Topolos at Russian River Vineyards

Apple Blossoms

Gravenstein Inn, Built 1872

85

Depot and Hotel Freeman, 1910
Courtesy, Sonoma County Library

This peaceful, colorful little community is home to a number of large respectful wineries though the feeling is of an earlier age. Once a major tourist draw to the natural geysers and hot springs in the eastern hills during the mid-1800's, Geyserville was originally called Clairville Station. The geysers fame mandated the name change and eventually they became one of only a few geothermal power developments in the world. Wine grapes occupy much of the rich alluvial soil throughout Alexander Valley now, including Asti, a winery village created as a cooperative community in the 1880's.

And Asti

Westward Aerial View of Geyserville

Westward Aerial View of Asti

Hope-Bosworth House, Built 1904

Hope-Merrill House, Built 1872

Chateau Souverain Winery

Downtown Buildings

Jack London Village

Founded in the 1850's by Frenchman Joshua Chauvet and established for flour production in the grist mill that today houses the Jack London Village, Glen Ellen has become an area that pays homage to it's most famous citizen, the American writer Jack London. Much of the town is a cherished memorial to the man who was the acclaimed writer of his day, though he prided himself as much a farmer, traveler and more, his legacy proves him justified. Wineries and a micro-brewery are popular destinations for today's visitor. Kenwood is the neighbor to the north resting at the base of Sugarloaf Ridge. Vineyards cover the land here with some prestigious wineries, large and small. Both communities have a number of small shops, B & B's and recreational opportunities including Morton's Warm Springs Park, hot air balloon rides, and several scenic regional parks.

Main St. and Kenwood Hotel, 1912
Courtesy, Sonoma County Library

GLEN ELLEN
ELEVATION - 279 FEET
TO SAN FRANCIS 59 M.

And Kenwood

Downtown Glen Ellen

Jack London State Park

Chateau St. Jean

Kenwood Depot

Old Winery Wall at Jack London State Park

Adobe Creek

Landmark Vineyards

GUERNEVILLE

...and then there's Guerneville!. Unique pristine scenery that includes the towering Redwood Trees, the Russian River and easy access to the coast all tucked into beautiful rolling hills and valleys, with pockets of vineyards and orchards. Once an elite get-away location for San Francisco's wealthy, many opulent and majestic hotels and lodges were built in the late 1800's after the area had been "discovered". Most of the grandiose establishments would succumb to the occasional harsh winter elements or a number of fires, accidental and natural, that have scarred the area several times. Guerneville's year-round community has had to rebound lately from the repeated flooding of the river, though with each flood, everyone pitches in to clean-up and the town is always prepared for the influx of the seasonal crowds. This is a popular resort area with an amazing diversity of people and events, there's a little bit of everything and everyone here at some point, a playground for the masses and the reclusive.

Northward Aerial View

Stumptown Daze Parade

Vineyards and Redwoods at Sunset

Russian River at Guernewood Park

Johnsons Beach

12 people in the cut-out of an old-growth Coast Redwood Tree in 1882. Courtesy, The Sonoma County Library

Jazz Festival

Armstrong Woods

Korbel Winery

A resort town hugging both banks of the Russian River, this area is home to the exclusive Bohemian Grove private resort and the former site of numerous luxury summer resorts, most of which were also destroyed by floods or fires over the last century. The current town includes a small year-round community with a large public beach , a revitalized amphitheater, a golf course and a number of nice inns and restaurants to accommodate the swell of the summer-time crowds that frequent the area.

Monte Rio, 1902
Courtesy, Sonoma County Library

Similar angle as above, note the regrowth of Redwoods

St. Catherine's

View from The Village Inn

Highland Dell Inn, Built 1906

Southward Aerial View of Monte Rio

Nestled in the redwoods thirteen miles from the coast rests this little historic town. Any one of five unique country roads will lead to Occidental, which was originally known as Howard's Station and boasted of its unique turntable for the areas trains and in producing 15,000 board feet of lumber a day in 1866. Rumors of past bootlegging and stills in the hills during prohibition lend an intriguing element to the town today. Fine Italian dining, quaint shops and pleasant accommodations exist much as they did in the late 1800's.

Southeastern Aerial View of Occidental

Negri's

St. Philip's Church

Downtown Shops

Inn at Occidental, Built 1877

Union Hotel, Built 1879

89

Welcome to
ROHNERT PARK

WELCOME to COTATI
The Hub of Sonoma County

One of the first "planned" communities in the U.S. in layout, design and structure, the town was incorporated in 1962. Formerly just flat open space as part of the original Rancho Cotate, the area was then developed as a seed farm by the Rohnert family. The first house was not even built until 1957 and now the area is growing rapidly with some major new developments. The California Welcome Center and the Sonoma County Wineries Association are here as well as the Crushers, a class AA professional baseball team, and a preforming arts center, a large theater complex, Hewlett-Packard, Sonoma State University, golf courses and the Crane Creek Regional Park. KRCB-TV is also based here.

California Welcome Center

View of Cotati, 1911
Courtesy, Sonoma County Library

Cotati was also part of the original Rancho Cotate who's namesake was kept in honor of a Miwok Indian tribe leader, Chief Kotate. This site is one of only two hexagonal parks in the United States. Cotati bills itself as the "Hub of Sonoma County", and its blend of funkiness and modernism is seen in old rustic barns and new commercial and industrial developments. Home of the popular jazz and accordion festivals, the town was originally settled in 1828 and first known as Page's Station but it was not incorporated until 1963. Approximately 6,700 people make their home here now.

Jazz Festival

Sonoma State University

Aerial of Rohnert Park and Cotati.
Downtown Cotati is in the center.

Scandia Fun Center

Downtown Cotati

Spreckels Performing Arts Center

Sam Berry's Livery Stable, Janssen's Hotel and Hall, 1885
Courtesy, Sonoma County Library

Formerly "Annaly", "Analy Township", and "Pine Grove", the current-day Sebastopol was settled in 1852. This is apple country! Over 7,500 residents proudly make their home in this town with agricultural history in becoming the Gravenstein Apple capital of the world. Still very popular are the annual Apple Blossom Festival and the Gravenstein Apple Fair celebrations. A premium wine growing region has also developed, along with numerous independent farms producing a wide range of items from blueberries and raspberries to pumpkins and christmas trees. The old-fashioned downtown and many neighborhoods contain elegant victorians. A very strong presence of antique dealers and collections are also here. The arts, llamas, a buddhist temple, a micro-brewery and the restored 1917 railroad depot which houses the West County Museum each add a slice of personality to this bustling small community.

Vineyards at Dehlinger Winery

Christmas Tree Farms

Northeast Aerial View

Apple Blossom Parade
and
Downtown Buildings

Apple Trees, Spring and Fall

The fastest growing community and most recently incorporated city, Windsor was established by Hiram Lewis of England in 1854 and is named after the visually similar oak studded countryside near Windsor Castle in England. This "gateway to the wine country" has grown to include over 19,000 residents. Expanded housing, commercial and retail developments are evident on both sides of the highway. Incorporated in 1992, the town now has a 18-hole golf course, a waterworks play park, campgrounds, vineyards and farms. The annual hot air balloon race and the world championship croquet tournaments are held here.

WINDSOR
Welcomes You

Martinelli Vineyards and Winery

Heritage Tree #4, Esposti Park

Balloon Race

Country Meadow Inn, Built 1896

Boyes Hot Springs

Fulton

Hacienda

Penngrove

North Coast Border of Sea Ranch and Gualala

Watson School District near Freestone

93

In getting to the place of bringing this book into print many people have been helpful on many levels. The most obvious reason this book was possible is the generous dealing and negotiations and patience and quality of the good people at Dexter who have brought my projects to life over the last six years. Randy, Christine, Jeanne, Louise, Nora, John, Bob, Don, Diane, Dwayne, Bruce and crew, you folks have been great partners in my difficult publications and the works we have produced would have just remained jumbled colored ideas bouncing around my brain without your services. Special thanks to all my retail and commercial clients (many shown photographically in this book within the communities section, though no one paid to be included in this pubication). Many thanks to the models who appear in the book; Jaga Dakota White (pages 20 & 50), Jeff Wright (page 20), Kendra and William Penn (pages 51 & 81), Melissa Mordecai and Martin Quinlan (page 75), Jennifer Owens (page 88), Romy Payne (page 89) and Laura Savage...thanks for these lips!. The Sonoma County Library's annex is to be commended for maintaining a vast collection of historical photographs and gave kind permission to use the historical photographs contained in this book. Many good people have been working for the betterment of Sonoma County for years and while I am apolitical in daily life, many of the dealings in keeping a whole county running as smoothly as possible fall on political decisions and those involved in the decisions, which in no way can ever please everyone. I would like to recognize some people for the positive work they have done for the county that quite often goes unnoticed or sometimes may even get too much attention, nonetheless I think these people and organizations have tried to make a difference in the county; Ernie Carpenter, Mike Riley and the current Board of Supervisors, Lynn Woolsey, Sonoma Land Trust, The Agricultural Preservation and Open Space District, Kay Marquet and the Sonoma County Community Foundation, Jean and Charles Schulz, Lori Moore at the City of Healdsburg, Don Test and Opal Pullaro at the Russian River Region Visitors Bureau, Jenny Carroll, Jamie Douglas, Linda Johnson, Chris Finley, Jessica Vann Gardner and Sondra Costello at the Petaluma Visitors Program, Keith Woods, The Greater Santa Rosa Convention and Visitors Bureau, Joe Horak, Richard Charter, Barbara Harris at the Cultural Art Council, Betsy Timm and Select Sonoma County, Sara Lee Kunde, Betsy Fisher, Elizabeth Slater, Clare Harris at Johnson's Beach, Millie Howie, Brenda Adelman, Michelle Wakeham at the Sonoma County Fairgrounds, and the SCCVB (rip). Special personal thanks to; Lyndi Brown for the "Taste of Sonoma County" text, Jack Wolf at Wolf Communications, the Martinelli Family and staff, the 5:14 and :45 seconds p.m. crew at Federal Express for only locking the door on me several times during the constant rush to send out the materials for this publication, Matthew Arnet and crew at KXFX radio, The towns of Monte Rio and Duncans Mills, the City of Cotati, Jim Ford at Fifth Resource Group, Linda Brown and Joan Trimble at the Cloverdale Chamber, the quality work of The Lab, the boy's at Unruh's Photography, Shutterbug Camera, Alpha Color Lab, Elisabeth and staff at Kits/Ritz Camera. Special thanks to; Alex Macondray for the initial design assistance and technical support during my month-long crash course in computer design education (Mazi, you've got a good `pa) and all the good folks at Kinko's Santa Rosa...Nathan, Morgan, Vigil, Christopher, Michael, Aaron, Alex, Leonard, Brian, Paul, Zoe and all you others there at my home-away-from-office, the fine ladies at the Healdsburg Inn on the Plaza, Compumotor, Multi-Contact, Hewlett-Packard, Cameron and Cameron, Team LP for that blast of energy every time you cruise past my office door, and a big heavy duty mushy thank you to my Tactical Air Support, ie... my aerial service providers... Arthur, Nancy and Kendall at Unique Travel Adventures for such great access to our friendly skies, George Zastrow, and that British guy with the Helicopter, and the Dutch guy with the hot air...balloon. Many many Cheesy Poofs were enjoyed during this production...one of the few things I could count on for some relief...thank you boys. Thanks to the guys and girls who have appeared in my previous calendars. Thanks for the print support from the Sonoma Independent, the details in Sonoma Business Magazine, Paul Jaffe at Copperfield's for the books, the historical prowess of Gaye LeBaron's work over the years, and to Dr. Marty Griffin.

Special somber thanks to my remaining family, the very few people to see and have had to partially experience how very difficult and often imposing my pursuits have been over the years. We each have some very unpleasant stuff going on in life as I complete this in early 1999 and all I can do is hope that things work out and hope you can now appreciate the sacrifices that have finally lead to this worthwhile (hopefully) production.

"Every sunset which I witness
inspires me with the desire to go to a west
as distant and as fair as that into
which the sun goes down."

– Henry David Thoreau (1817-1862)
American Writer